Animal Life

Stephen Aitken

Cavendish Square

New York

Published in 2014 by Cavendish Square Publishing, LLC
303 Park Avenue South, Suite 1247, New York, NY 10010

Library of Congress Cataloging-in-Publication Data
Aitken, Stephen, 1953-
Climate crisis — animal life / Stephen Aitken.
    p. cm.
Includes bibliographical references and index.
Summary: "Provides information on how climate change affects animal life"—Provided by publisher.
ISBN 978-1-60870-459-0 (hardcover)
ISBN 978-1-62712-039-5 (paperback)
ISBN 978-1-60870-630-3 (ebook)
1. Climatic changes. 2. Climatic changes—Environmental aspects. I. Title.
QC903.15.A58 2012
591.72'2—dc22
2010025668

Editor: Megan Comerford
Art Director: Anahid Hamparian
Series Designer: Nancy Sabato

Photo research by Laurie Platt Winfrey, Carousel Research, Inc.

Cover photo: Getty Images: Rinie Van Meurs/Foto Natura/Minden Pictures

The photographs in this book are used by permission and through the courtesy of:
Alamy: Eureka, 10; Chris Wallace, 23; Ricardo Jamin, 24-25; Foto Natura, 27; Stone Nature Photography, 28; Robert Fried, 33; Thomas Kitchin & Victoria Hurst/First Light, 37; Jason Edwards/National Geographic Images, 42. *AP Photo*: Pavel Rahman, 30-31. *Getty Images*: Jim Brandenburg/ Minden Pictures, 12-13; Jason Edwards/National Geographic Images, 38-39. *Glow Images*: Neotake, dry lake bed details; Schulz/F1online, 16. *Cavendish Square Publishing, LLC Royalty Free*: 4; 49. *Photo Researchers*: Alan Sirulnikoff, 41. *Photoshot*: Maurizio Valentini/NHPA, Titlepage + 18-19. *Superstock*: Cultura Ltd Royalty Free, 60-61.

Printed in the United States of America

Contents

Introduction

limate change on our planet has the ability to impact all living organisms and their environments, no matter how remote or distant those environments are from human development, whether on land, under the sea, or in the air. That is why climate change is the greatest threat to wildlife on our planet today.

For more than 3.5 billion years our atmosphere has sustained life-supporting conditions on Earth—the only known haven for life in the universe. We don't know exactly when human beings started affecting the atmosphere on a large scale. Some researchers say it was when agriculture became a widespread practice; others think it was at the time of the Industrial Revolution, with the invention of the steam engine. The fact is, human beings have gradually gained dominance over the land and, to an increasing extent, over the sea.

Slowly but surely over the past century, the global temperature has risen due to carbon dioxide (CO_2) emissions from the burning of

"The exhalations of breath and other gaseous emissions by the nearly 7 billion people on Earth, their pets, and their livestock are responsible for 23 percent of all greenhouse gas emissions."

—JAMES LOVELOCK

A lion waits at a watering hole for prey to arrive.

fossil fuels and deforestation. According to a 2007 report published by the Intergovernmental Panel on Climate Change (IPCC), the leading body for the assessment of climate change, established by the United Nations, the global temperature rose 1.1 degrees Fahrenheit (0.6 degrees Celsius) during the twentieth century. Conservative predictions forecast another 3.2 to 7.2 °F (1.8 to 4.0 °C) rise this century. Some of the remotest areas, such as those near the poles, are warming at rates up to twice as fast as the rest of the world.

What impact does a warming climate have on living organisms and their **habitats**? The total number of species on Earth is estimated to be between 5 and 50 million—with fewer than 2 million species of animals, plants, and algae described and recorded by scientists to date. Our continents support more than 21,000 known species of **terrestrial** vertebrates—land animals with spinal columns—such as frogs, lizards, birds, and mammals. Climate change is having an impact on these animals as well as on their **ecosystems**.

Humans have made life difficult for land vertebrates through hunting and poaching and the wholesale destruction of their habitats. How can scientists possibly predict the effects of global warming when pollution, deforestation, agricultural expansion, urban development, and habitat destruction are all occurring simultaneously? The study of climate change requires the detective prowess of a Sherlock Holmes and the organizational skills of a Charles Darwin.

Since this is the first time in recorded history that we have actually witnessed human-induced climate change, scientists don't know all its possible impacts. Evidence from about 18,000 years ago, during the last glacial retreat, has given **climatologists** some idea of the types of migrations to expect in a warming climate. They predict that rising temperatures will result in many animals moving toward cooler, more suitable habitats. Many animals are expected to move away from the tropical regions toward higher latitudes (in the direction of the poles) as well as to climb to higher elevations—cooler mountainside climates. Species that are unable to move may be left staring into the brutal face of extinction.

An ecosystem includes not only the physical environment but also the species inhabiting a given area. Studies show that species are reacting to climate change in a variety of ways, and dramatic changes are taking place at a rapid rate. Will ecosystems be able to rebalance themselves and survive? This is a question many climate researchers and **ecologists** are asking themselves.

The study of ancient ecosystems, known as **paleoecology**, provides evidence that a warming climate drives changes in the geographic **ranges** of animals, but different species within communities do not necessarily undergo similar range shifts. The timing of a range shift is determined by each species' sensitivity to climate change. Factors affecting species' sensitivity include physical mobility, life span, and the availability of needed resources such as food, water, and shelter.

The effects of climate change on different species can result in the breakup of existing ecosystems and the formation of new ones, with unknown consequences. Many scientists believe that climate change will become the most significant cause of **biodiversity** loss in this century. Many species will have difficulty adapting quickly enough or integrating smoothly into new environments due to the rapid rate of change.

The natural functioning of the environment provides both goods and services on which our society depends. For example, ecosystems store great amounts of the chemical element carbon (C) in plants and soils, helping to reduce **greenhouse gases**, such as CO_2. Ecosystems also regulate water flow and improve water quality, provide food and nutrients, and regulate floods and disease. Healthy ecosystems stabilize local climates and maintain the conditions required for life on Earth.

These services, however, are made possible by only natural ecosystem processes: photosynthesis, the process by which plants capture CO_2 from the atmosphere and create new growth; the plant and soil processes that recycle nutrients from decomposing matter and keep the soil fertile; and the processes by which plants draw water from soils and return water to the atmosphere. These ecosystem processes are affected by climate and by the concentration of CO_2 in the atmosphere. Biodiversity is itself an important resource that maintains ecosystem balance, provides goods, and enhances ecosystem services.

The dramatic ecosystem changes taking place at higher latitudes and in the polar regions have largely overshadowed the effects of warming on tropical animals. But tropical climates have also been warming—more than 1.4 °F (0.8 °C) since 1975—and according to some climate models, the tropical forests of Central and South America will warm more than 5.5 °F (3 °C) during this century. Scientists expect this to result in temperature zones shifting close to 2,000 feet (600 meters) uphill. This most likely means that some tropical species will also move to these higher elevations in an effort to stay in suitable climate zones.

Infectious Diseases

Many epidemiologists (scientists who study the spread of diseases in human populations and environments) believe that climate change will increase the occurrence of insect-borne diseases. Malaria, dengue fever, and **viral encephalitides**, such as West Nile virus, are all diseases that are spread by mosquitoes. Warmer temperatures are expected to increase the mosquitoes' geographical ranges and their biting and reproductive rates, as well as shorten the **incubation period** of the **pathogens** they carry. Climate change is expected to lead to an increase in UV radiation, which could cause decreased food production and might weaken the human immune system. Malnutrition in some populations may also leave people more susceptible to insect-borne diseases. All of these factors taken together do not bode well for human or animal health in a warming climate.

Invasive Species

Invasive species are an additional stress on ecosystems. Human actions (accidentally introducing non-native species) and rising temperatures, which have forced species to seek more suitable habitats, have resulted in an increase in the number of invasive species. The most harmful invasive plants appear to tolerate a wider range of environmental conditions and may very well find a warming world even more hospitable. The number of invasive animal species is expected to increase as well, as animals look for cooler, more suitable habitats. If this trend continues, native plant and animal species, as well as natural ecosystems, will be threatened.

The Burmese python, popular among reptile owners, can become a dangerous invasive species if released into the wild.

Ecosystems of the Future

Global warming is expected to create entirely new **biomes** and landscapes, the likes of which have never been seen. The future climate in many areas on Earth may be entirely different from current conditions. The regions most vulnerable to major biome shifts are around the equator, where tropical rain forests will be taken over by savannas, replacing lush trees with rolling fields of tall grass. According to some reports, the Sahara desert may get even hotter.

TIME TO ACT fact!

Climate-induced droughts are leading to more frequent bushfires and habitat loss for the Indonesian orangutan. The survival of this intelligent primate may be at risk due to the increasing isolation of populations.

The grey wolf needs a large area to hunt in. Habitat destruction, encounters with humans, and now climate change have all impacted its population size.

Chapter One

The Race for Survival

If only a few species were to exhibit the migrations that scientists predicted, it might be considered a coincidence; a few dozen incidents could indicate a broad pattern of change. But in fact, a study of more than 1,500 species from around the world showed that no fewer than 800 species have responded to recent warming trends by shifting their ranges toward cooler climates. Such numbers make it impossible to dismiss these findings as coincidental. Range shifts are being observed by ecologists and other scientists over and over again, leaving little doubt that climate change is having a powerful impact on determining where specific land vertebrates can survive in our warming world.

Studies have shown that animals living at higher latitudes are moving farther than those at lower latitudes. This may be due in part to the fact that polar regions are warming at a faster rate than the rest of the world, with the Arctic warming at double the average global rate. Climate scientists predict that during this century, animals will need to move an average of a quarter mile (400 m) a year to escape habitats that have become unsuitable due to climate change.

The distance animals need to move may also depend on the **topography** of the area in which they live. For species that live in flatter, low-lying regions such as deserts, grasslands, and coastal regions, the "retreat from the heat" could be more than a half mile (800 m) annually. Those animals unable to make the shift quickly enough could become extinct. Species survival may ultimately depend on the ability of animals to keep pace with changing climates.

Not all animals have to travel long distances to reach cooler climates. Since temperatures are lower at higher elevations, nearby mountains can provide animals with access to cooler habitats. But animals that move to these alpine areas may literally run out of room. If global warming increases to the point where the mountaintop is no longer habitable, animals may become trapped, with nowhere else to go. This phenomenon is referred to as the "summit trap," and extinction is often the result.

A recent study in Madagascar revealed that thirty species of reptiles and amphibians shifted their habitats uphill by as much as 175 feet (53 m) between 1993 and 2003.

Birds

Birds are an important part of many ecosystems because of their role in seed dispersal, pollination, and as both predator and prey in the food chain.

Birds have a big advantage in being able to take flight in response to predators and changing habitats. Many birds can migrate long distances to reach suitable climates. Partly due to this mobility, birds provide early warnings of environmental change.

Many North American birds are shifting their ranges in response to warming climates. According to studies by researchers at the State University of New York College of Environmental Science and Forestry (ESF) that compare historical atlases of bird ranges to current data, the southern boundaries of many bird ranges have shifted northward. Some of the species making this southern boundary shift are the Nashville warbler, a little bird with a yellow belly; the pine siskin, a common finch that resembles a sparrow; and the red-bellied woodpecker, considered the most common woodpecker in the Southeast. The shifts have occurred in a matter of just decades, some by as much as 40 miles (64 kilometers), and are consistent with the predictions of regional warming.

Many European bird migrations are likely to get longer—by as much as 250 miles (400 km), according to a study done by researchers at Durham University in England. This is bad news for birds such as the common whitethroat, which weighs less than half an ounce (14 grams). Birds have to put on a lot of fat before migrating long distances; some even shrink their internal organs to become more fuel efficient. The need for longer migrations could threaten their very survival.

In tropical areas, birds tend to be highly specialized, with smaller habitat ranges. This makes them more vulnerable to habitat destruction from deforestation or urban development. The smaller ranges can leave them homeless and may lead to extinction of the species.

Pikas—Heading for the Peaks

The pika is a tiny, hamster-size mammal that lives in the mountainous regions of the western United States. It does not like the heat. As temperatures rise, the pika is scurrying farther up the mountain slopes. A 2003 study showed that more than one-third of the twenty-five known pika populations have already disappeared.

If daytime temperatures are too high, the pika will not **forage** for food.

Experiments show that air temperatures of 78 °F (25.5 °C) are fatal for the pika. Further troubling is the fact that the western United States is slated to have some of the most significant temperature changes in the country— a summertime increase of 5.4 °F (3 °C) in the pika's current range by 2050.

Environmental organizations have sued the federal government to protect the pika under the Endangered Species Act. They argue that legal action is the only way to force the government to protect the pika.

In February 2010 the U.S. Fish and Wildlife Service declared that the pika was not an endangered species. It claimed that only some populations were declining, while others were not. Some people feel that this little fur ball has now become a political football.

At least four hundred species of birds could become endangered in the next forty years—and these are species not currently at risk. Birds that migrate long distances are particularly vulnerable, since several climate zones are involved. Migratory birds, for instance, may return to their northern ranges to find that spring has come early. This might mean that, after breeding, their young may have missed the peak insect cycles that would have provided them with food for growth and development. Also, birds that relocate to more suitable habitats due to climate-induced change may find that their prey and preferred food sources are not available. Scientists are only beginning to learn how climate change alters the timing of **ecological interactions**, but many suspect that the cross-species impacts are going to be significant.

Observations made over more than one hundred years indicate that global warming is having an impact on the natural cycles within these ecosystems. There are many indications that spring is arriving earlier every year. If the warming trend continues, many ecosystems may be weakened further, threatening their ability to support the many species that rely on them.

TIME TO ACT fact!

Audubon's 2008 Christmas Bird Count revealed that 58 percent of the 305 widespread species that winter on the North American continent have shifted significantly north since 1968—some by as much as 100 miles (160 km).

Spanish brown bears in the Cordilleran Mountains are foregoing hibernation altogether due to warmer winter weather.

Chapter Two

Timing Is Everything

Key life-cycle events, such as reproduction, hibernation, and migration, are slowly shifting in response to global warming. In the United States, spring now arrives, on average, ten days to two weeks earlier than it did in 1990.

A study of northeastern birds that migrate long distances has found that birds wintering in the southern United States now arrive back in the Northeast an average of thirteen days earlier than they did during the first half of the twentieth century. Birds wintering in South America arrive back in the Northeast an average of four days earlier. Scientists have observed that in recent years, birds are also breeding and laying their eggs earlier.

Rising spring temperatures along the east coast of the United States have led to earlier nesting for twenty-eight migratory bird species. Many migratory species have also changed their wintering habitats, and some have changed critical stopover habitats.

Research shows that many small mammals are coming out of hibernation earlier than they did several decades ago, and others are changing their breeding patterns in response to the warmer climate. Some studies show that bears, particularly females with young cubs, are sometimes foregoing hibernation altogether.

According to studies on hibernating ground squirrels, warmer winter temperatures are causing another problem: hibernating species are running out of energy before spring. Higher temperatures result in stored fat reserves being used at a faster rate. The depletion of these reserves can cause hibernating animals to awaken early, placing some species fatally "out of sync" with their environment. According to Italian scientists, for instance, dormice, famous for their six-month siestas, are hibernating five weeks less than they did just two decades ago. An early wake-up might not be a problem if plenty of food is waiting just outside the den. But animals roused from hibernation by warmer temperatures in late winter or early spring may find nature's cupboard bare.

Two of the more important and well documented effects of climate change on **phenology** (see page 22) are changes in the date of plant flowering and disruptions of existing food chains. Important life-cycle events in plants and animals are often interrelated, meaning that one event may trigger the occurrence of another. When the timing of these events changes, the balance within an ecosystem can be thrown off.

SPANISH BROWN BEARS

Bears are supposed to hibernate throughout the winter, when the frozen hills make food hard to find. Traditionally, they slow their metabolisms to a minimum and draw on stored resources, losing up to 40 percent of their body weight before they become active again in the warm spring weather.

A study has shown that some bears have stopped hibernating altogether in the mountains of northern Spain. The cordillera is home to an estimated 130 bears that are genetically unique (unlike the world's other bear populations). The study, by Spain's Brown Bear Foundation, reported that many females and young cubs in this region have remained active throughout recent winters. Warming winter weather has resulted in sparse snow cover and a plentiful supply of nuts and berries. The mature males, which still enjoy their winter slumber, are exhibiting shorter hibernation periods every year.

This study in itself does not prove that climate change is the reason Spanish bears are foregoing their hibernation. However, the change in hibernation is consistent with expected climate-change results and indicates that climate change may have many other unknown impacts on the natural world.

A Phenomenon Called Phenology

Fruit trees blossom when warm spring weather arrives, and animals give birth at a time when food is abundant for their young. These and other key life-cycle events in plants, insects, and animals are initiated by variations in the climate.

Phenology is the study of these life-cycle events and their relationship to climate. This information is important for scientists investigating the impact of climate change on ecosystems and living organisms.

For example, the date that flowers bloom controls the timing of allergens and infectious diseases—impacting human health. Timing is everything when it comes to ecosystem balance and species survival.

A caribou fawn takes a well-needed break on a patch of soft summer grass.

For example, nectar-producing trees in the northeastern United States are blooming several weeks earlier than they did in the past. Honeybees are now getting nectar from the black locust tree rather than from their previous source, the tulip poplar tree. Some scientists believe this is affecting the pollination of tulip poplars and causing a dramatic decline in the tree's population.

Some large animals are also at risk due to changes in phenology. Arctic caribou used to give birth when plants were at their peak and readily available. However, climate change has affected the timing of these two events so that caribou births are no longer occurring when plant food is readily available. This has resulted in a 400-percent increase in the death rate of newly born caribou.

Some plant and animal species may benefit from climate change, while others, such as the tulip poplar and the caribou, may suffer. However, an earlier spring means that flowering plants will bloom earlier, likely leading to more ecosystem imbalance.

Arctic fox populations are declining due to climate-related impacts. Fewer than two hundred individuals remain in Scandinavia.

Chapter Three

The Planet of the Small

In addition to impacting the complex interactions between species and life-cycle events, climate change appears to be affecting the physical development and anatomy of individual organisms. Scientists have noticed that vertebrates are getting smaller as temperatures rise. Studies of aquatic species indicate a body-size reduction linked to global warming, as well as a decrease in the number of juvenile (not fully developed) animals present within populations.

Ecologists have long been aware of the tendency of warmer environments to be dominated by smaller-size species, but until now that phenomenon has not been directly equated with climate change. Research indicates that, over time, animal communities in warmer environments tend toward smaller average body sizes. This size reduction has been noted across different ecosystems and in different kinds of organisms, indicating that global warming does have a real effect on size.

The trend toward smaller organisms can take place on one or more levels of the population. Being small may mean that an organism belongs to a small-size species that has become more successful due to global warming, or that the average age of individuals within a population is younger so the average size is smaller, or that the organism is indeed small for its age due to the negative effect of higher temperatures on its physical development.

Studies have long shown that birds and other animals living closer to the poles tend to be larger than those of the same, or similar, species living nearer the equator. Scientists believe this phenomenon is an adaptation to heat stress, since a larger body is more difficult to keep cool. In biology there is a general rule of thumb, known as **Bergmann's Rule**, that says individuals within a species, or within closely related species, tend to be smaller in warmer climates.

This may be due to a number of reasons. For one thing, a smaller body has a proportionally larger surface area for the dissipation of heat.

LITTLE LAMBS

Milder winters are causing Scotland's wild Soay sheep to get smaller. The sheep, which live on the island of Hirta, have been decreasing in size since 1985. Researchers have concluded that the decrease in body size is primarily a response to environmental variation—in other words, the warming weather.

More specifically, lambs are not growing as quickly as they once did. As winters have become shorter and milder, lambs do not need to put on as much weight in the first months of life in order to survive until their first birthday.

Even the slower-growing lambs now have a chance of surviving. The results highlight how wide ranging the effects of global climate change can be, adding another important factor to monitor in natural populations in the future.

Many North American songbirds are gradually becoming smaller.
The Scarlet Tanager is more than 2 percent smaller today than fifty years ago.

Other factors may also play a role, including the availability of food and the organism's **metabolic rate** (the rate at which it burns calories, which in turn determines how much food the organism requires).

A study of almost half a million birds belonging to more than one hundred species shows that songbirds in the United States are getting smaller. Many are gradually becoming lighter and are growing shorter wings. This shrinkage has occurred within just half a century and is believed to be a response to warmer temperatures. The body-size variation has occurred over a period of twenty generations or more.

The forty-six-year study showed that springtime-migrating birds declined in size an average of only 1.3 percent, which is quite a small change. However, the decline in body size for some species was much greater. The rose-breasted grosbeak, for example, lost about 4 percent of its weight, while the Kentucky warbler dropped 3.3 percent and the scarlet tanager dropped 2.3 percent. The trend toward smaller sizes was particularly evident in birds that winter in the Caribbean, Central America, South America, and the New World tropics.

The changes in body size do not appear to be restricted to North American birds. Some Australian birds have adapted to rising temperatures with reduced body sizes as well. Other studies have found similar trends of shrinking birds and mammals in Great Britain, Denmark, Israel, and New Zealand.

Experts estimate that the number of tigers in the wild is as low as 3,200 individuals. Rising sea levels in the mangrove forests of India could put populations there at risk of extinction.

Chapter Four

Animals Under Fire

The vertebrates most vulnerable to climate change are those with a **physiology** sensitive to small changes in temperature or moisture. They are in grave danger; many species may soon be staring into the grim face of extinction.

It takes many generations for a species to adapt. Adaptation by natural selection means that individuals with physical traits and behaviors that are advantageous in an altered habitat—which may include new predators and new food sources—survive to pass those traits on to their offspring.

However, adaptation by species selection typically happens over a long period of time. Biodiversity has developed over hundreds of millions of years. But the sheer speed of global climate change is making it very difficult for species to adapt at a pace that will ensure their survival.

It was 1987 in the Monteverde Cloud Forest Reserve when American ecologist Martha Crump first sighted the spectacular golden toad's mating ritual around puddles on the forest floor. Little did she know that within only a couple of years, the golden toad would become the first documented victim of climate change.

An explanation for its disappearance was not put forth until a decade later. Warming Pacific waters, caused by El Niño and made worse by global warming, had altered the golden toad's habitat, making it drier. The tropical habitat had been kept moist—and therefore livable for the golden toad and other species—by a low-hanging mist. The change in ocean temperature caused the mist to rise above the level of the forest, causing the habitat to dry out. This change of habitat, coupled with a lethal amphibian disease caused by the chytrid fungus, created a situation that the golden toad could no longer survive. It wasn't long before the last of its breeding puddles had dried up, and the golden toad was no more than a golden memory.

Researchers have watched other amphibian species vanish for similar reasons all over the world. Two species of anoles, small relatives of iguanas, also vanished from the same area in Monteverde around the same time as

 The first suspected victim of climate change, the extinct golden toad, was once abundant in the high altitude cloud forests near Monteverde, Costa Rica.

the golden toad. The mountain's cloud forests continue to be stripped of their fauna (wildlife), with many species becoming rarer by the year.

In the early 1970s the discovery of the gastric brooding frog in Australia astonished field biologists. As they looked into a female's open mouth, they saw a tiny frog sitting on her tongue. At first they thought the mother frog was eating her young, but on closer inspection, they discovered that a unique breeding behavior had evolved in which the female swallows her fertilized eggs. The tadpoles develop in the mother's stomach and then metamorphose (change) into tiny frogs, which are then regurgitated into the world.

Medical researchers were anxious to study how the female frog transformed its stomach from an acidic digestion chamber into a life-supporting nursery. They had hoped that uncovering this mystery might help them cure a variety of stomach ailments in humans. But alas, nine years after its discovery, the gastric brooding frog vanished from its **desiccated** habitat, taking its brooding mystery with it—another suspected victim of global warming.

More than six thousand known amphibian species exist in the animal kingdom, and moisture is vital for the survival of each and every one of them. But rising temperatures are drying out many of their habitats and leading to an increase in amphibian diseases—resulting in a rapid increase in adult mortality.

In North America, research on the genus *Bufo* (toads) uncovered the fact that ultraviolet (UV) light hinders the development of the toad's embryos (the very early developmental stage of an organism). This makes them more susceptible to the fungal disease *Saprolegnia ferax*, a killer of amphibians worldwide. Ponds in which the toads lay their eggs are shallower on average because the increased global temperature leads to faster evaporation of pond water. Shallower nursery ponds result in more UV light hitting the embryos. In the worst-case scenarios, the ponds dry up entirely, killing all of the tadpoles. Once again, climate change is a prime suspect in the rising amphibian extinction rate.

Scientists with the IPCC have used current trends in carbon emissions to estimate how significant the temperature increase in the twenty-first century will be. If global temperatures increase 3.2 to 5.2 °F (1.8 to 2.9 °C) above current levels—which is the IPCC's most optimistic prediction—20 to 30 percent of species will be in climate zones that are far outside of their current ranges. This will place them at risk of extinction. The IPCC's more pessimistic prediction estimates that global temperatures could increase by 7.2 to 11.5 °F (4 to 6.4°C). A temperature change of this magnitude would have a devastating effect on animals and their ecosystems.

Reptiles

The success of reptiles in adapting to changes in climate may depend on their ability to slither to more suitable habitats. Some species of North American salamanders lay their eggs in temporary pools formed from melting snow in the spring. A warmer, drier climate may cause these ponds to evaporate earlier in the season, impacting salamander populations.

Habitat changes are occurring not only in North America but also worldwide. Studies in Madagascar show that thirty species of reptiles and amphibians searching for cooler habitats have fled uphill in a race against the rising mercury.

Scientists predict that at least three species of reptiles will become extinct between 2050 and 2100 on a mountaintop in Madagascar due to the summit-trap phenomenon. If rising temperatures keep forcing the reptiles higher up the mountains, they will eventually run out of land. The extinction of many of the world's mountain-dwelling species is inevitable if temperatures continue to rise.

These are some other animals threatened by climate change.

- **Flamingos** are strongly affected by declines in the availability and quality of their wetland habitat in the Caribbean, South America, Asia, and Africa.

- **White-lipped peccaries**, mammals living in Central and South America, depend on shallow ponds to survive during the region's dry season.

- **Bicknell's thrushes**, birds that breed and nest high on mountains in northeastern North America, are facing shrinking habitats due to the effects of industrial pollution on the trees in which they nest.

- **Chirus (Tibetan antelope)**, which dwell on the high Tibetan Plateau, face climate change as well as increased human development in their habitat.

- **Irrawaddy dolphins**, native to Southeast Asia, suffer from habitat degradation.

- **Lemmings**, small rodents that live near the Arctic, are contending with altered breeding habitats that are no longer providing the creatures with enough food, warmth, or protection.

 Buff-breasted sandpipers, which breed along the western coast of North America and winter in South America, are potentially at risk if pollution continues to harm their habitats.

 Wolverines, mammals that live in cold climates in the Northern Hemisphere, are threatened by warming temperatures, which alter their habitats, making the young more vulnerable to predators.

Wolverine numbers are falling due to warmer temperatures, along with the amount and persistence of the snowfall.

Low precipitation levels coupled with overgrazing can lead to the loss of vegetation and soils, ultimately causing desertification.

Chapter Five

Linking Conservation and Climate

The movement to conserve biodiversity and ecosystems has a long history. More than 12 percent of Earth's land surface is currently protected, including 100,000 parks, nature reserves, and marine areas. But are these areas designed to protect species and their habitats in a world of rapidly changing climate? Sadly, the answer is no.

Plants and animals need the opportunity to move toward their temperature comfort zones and new habitats when the conditions of their previous habitats have changed. The fixed boundaries of the world's protected areas are not designed for this movement nor for the impacts on species and ecosystems of climate change. We must plan for the climatic conditions of fifty to one hundred years from now and beyond.

Protected Areas and Biolink Zones

Protected areas will need to be expanded and/or joined together to form larger networks within which species can move if their previous habitats become unsuitable. Studies have shown that **biolink zones**, which may include wildlife corridors, can provide pathways for wildlife, plants, and insects to move along so they can recolonize (populate new areas with colonies of individuals) more suitable habitats. Ideally, all of the protected areas on a continent should be connected (with additional protected zones) to allow for maximum mobility of species in a changing climate and to prevent individual populations from remaining isolated and therefore becoming more vulnerable to the pressures of change.

Large protected areas can slow species extinctions, but they cannot prevent them if populations and habitats become isolated as the climate changes. Dispersal (the movement of individuals into new areas) and recolonization are essential components of the process of evolution. Many species have traditionally moved between habitats, between summering and wintering grounds, and to and from birthing sites. Human-made alterations to the natural landscape—urban development, freeways, agricultural areas, and deforestation—slow or constrict the free movement of species.

A wildlife corridor in the form of an overpass allows species to cross over an expressway.

Protected areas have been developed to attempt to conserve wildlife and their habitats while at the same time allowing modern society to flourish.

Large, wide-ranging carnivores, such as wolves, bears, and wolverines, are at risk, particularly when they unknowingly leave protected areas while chasing prey or naturally dispersing into new areas when their populations become too large in their traditional habitats. Without biolinks, stressed ecosystems can collapse abruptly. The loss of a single **keystone species** (such as the wolf) can be disastrous for an ecosystem because of its large impact on populations and habitat in a given area.

THE TUNNEL OF LOVE

The mountain pygmy possum of Australia has been heavily impacted by global warming. Australians are very concerned with climate change and its effect on drought, fire, and flood regimes across the whole continent. The mountain pygmy possum, a small Australian mammal, lives only in the alpine-subalpine region. Ski resorts threaten the three distinct populations.

In 1986 a wildlife crossing was built on Mount Higginbotham. The intent was to restore a connection with one of the other populations that had been isolated by the construction of a road and a ski resort. The new crossing enabled males to travel to and mate with females. The crossing became known as the "tunnel of love."

Importantly, it allowed the young animals to disperse to other habitats, leaving the mothers to get fat for hibernation. Research indicates that the wildlife crossing had a positive effect on the health of the population, preventing what could have been local extinction. The community has remained healthy for more than twenty-five years.

More crossings were built in other locations where the pygmy possums were at extreme risk of extinction. This success is an example of how connecting habitats together through crossings and biolink zones can allow populations to adapt to the impacts of climate change.

Managers of protected areas and conservationists in southern Australia are actively planning and creating biolink zones that will allow wildlife to move between existing natural areas. The benefits of this free movement of species between connected ecosystems include healthier wildlife populations, increased diversity of species, and increased carbon storage. These all help to reduce the effects of climate change.

The success of a biolink depends to a great extent on the similarities between the two connected areas. In effect, the biolinked areas create a larger habitable area for wildlife, providing prey with more options for hiding from predators and increasing the diversity of places for species to reproduce and recolonize. Success also depends on the area surrounding a biolink. For example, a rural biolink has a greater chance of success than an urban corridor, because the likelihood of humans or domestic animals disrupting the linked zone is much lower in a rural area, where there are fewer humans and domestic animals.

There are also potential problems associated with biolinks. They can facilitate the spread of fire and disease from one area to another. Prey may become easier to catch if corridors are too narrow. Some managers of protected areas perceive the potential costs of establishing large-scale biolinks a huge obstacle.

However, the benefits of ecosystem services—such as increased carbon storage, improved water quality, and maintenance of biodiversity—that were salvaged by the establishment of a biolink need to be considered against the cost of land-use change. The restoration of the linked ecosystems and the species that live in them should increase the chances of a sustainable relationship between urban development and the natural world despite the pressures of a changing climate.

Even in urban ecosystems, links in the form of small paths of greenery connecting to surrounding rural areas can benefit wild bird and butterfly populations by creating refuges and areas for safe passage. These urban networks can also benefit from rooftop **biotopes**, which act as refuges for certain species during their movement between areas of urban greenery and larger areas in the continental landscape. An ideal plan for a conservation network is a well-established multipark network connecting many types of protected areas.

The International Union for Conservation of Nature (IUCN), an organization that unites many countries, government agencies, organizations, and scientists, has a huge goal. It hopes to create a continuous network of protected areas along the western mountain ranges, stretching from Argentina to Alaska.

Dealing with Desertification

One of the worst effects of rising temperatures may be prolonged and unforgiving droughts. More than 20 percent of the land on Earth is desert, but this percentage is increasing along with global temperatures. The constant presence in all the great deserts of the world is the sun. Unrelenting solar radiation evaporates desert water almost as quickly as it forms. When neither water nor food from plants is available, death quickly follows.

FROM YELLOWSTONE TO THE YUKON

The Yellowstone to Yukon Conservation Initiative, or Y2Y, is a joint Canada—United States not-for-profit organization that has taken on the responsibility of creating a continuous network of protected areas from Yellowstone National Park, located in Wyoming, Montana, and Idaho, to the Yukon Territory in northwestern Canada.

The organization's goal is to join all of the diverse conservation areas together to protect the native plants, wildlife, and wilderness of this entire region. Y2Y coordinates a network of organizations, agencies, and individuals doing on-the-ground conservation work to conserve the region's natural heritage for future generations. Learn more about Y2Y at www.y2y.net.

The story of a gray wolf named Pluie was one of the motivations for creating the Y2Y network. In 1991, collared with a satellite transmitter in Alberta, Pluie traveled through two Canadian provinces and three American states over the course of two years, demonstrating just how far and wide carnivores roam. Pluie's travels emphasized that many protected parks do not provide animals with adequate space. The establishment of biolinks is particularly important for the conservation of large carnivores, such as wolves.

Desert species have adapted to this water shortage through a wide range of fascinating specializations. One of the most common behaviors is nocturnal (nighttime) hunting and foraging, adopted by many desert animals to reduce their exposure to the heat of the sun.

The African Sahel region is the wide sweep of sub-Saharan land extending from the Atlantic Ocean in the west to Sudan in the east. The past fifty years have seen a decline in rainfall that has transformed this area from one of marginal precipitation into a near desert.

Through a detailed study by climatologists in 2003, researchers deduced that the principal cause was rising sea-surface temperatures in the Indian Ocean, one of the most rapidly warming oceans on Earth. They fear that the drought might continue throughout this century. Climatologists worry that the climate shift in this region is so severe, it could influence the climate of the entire planet. Drought conditions as they exist now in Africa and Australia may extend into southern Europe if temperatures keep rising.

Australia's southwestern region, once a place of predictable rainfall and substantial wheat and grape production, has seen a 15-percent decrease in rainfall. Crop production is suffering. Some researchers think the destruction of the ozone layer above Antarctica is one of the causes, drawing the southern rainfall zone even farther south.

Across the Pacific Ocean, much of the American West is experiencing long-term drought—the worst in the past seven hundred years. As with the African Sahel, some climatologists believe the drought is due to rising ocean temperatures, though IPCC scientists attribute the decrease in precipitation to increased temperatures over the land.

According to the U.S. Global Change Research Program, a reduction in the snowpack (the packed snow that forms in the winter months in areas of high altitude) is cutting summertime stream flow by 25 percent, with projected declines of as much as 40 percent by the 2040s. Fish habitats have been affected, but even more worrisome is the fact that warmer temperatures are melting the snow before it can consolidate, and the snowpack as a whole is melting earlier. The runoff into streams is happening approximately three weeks earlier than it was half a century ago. Given the projected temperature increases for this century, streams may eventually flow in the winter—when the water is least needed. Water supply could well be the biggest problem in the western United States in years to come.

The formation of new deserts, a process known as desertification, results in the loss of soil and vegetation. This, in turn, affects the global climate. The loss of vegetation from activities such as grazing leads to losses in **primary production** and ultimately to the inability of an area to absorb CO_2. High temperatures and low precipitation levels eventually lead to loss of drylands (ecosystems such as scrublands and savannas that are characterized by a lack of water), turning them into deserts. Associated with the loss of drylands is the loss of biodiversity and habitats, as well as the ecosystem services provided by the dryland ecosystem. Dryland soils converted into desert sand also means the loss of an important carbon sink. Climatologists fear that a major percentage of this carbon will be released back into the atmosphere as CO_2, increasing greenhouse-gas levels.

Rain Forest Loss

Rain forests are home to almost half of all animal and plant species on Earth. At the current rate of tree cutting, scientists predict that most of the world's rain forests will be gone by 2030, and half of the remaining forests will be in poor condition. Forests (including their soils) are a carbon sink, absorbing up to one-third of the extra CO_2 being added to the atmosphere.

Many rain-forest areas are hot spots of biodiversity. By protecting these areas, we can protect as many species as possible through one action. Every protection plan should take into account the needs of the local communities and indigenous peoples. Experience shows that these locally shared initiatives are very often the most successful.

Managed Relocations: Is it Time to Stop Resisting?

Endangered species whose traditional habitats have been degraded by climate change and other pressures can be relocated by scientists to more accommodating habitats. However, managed relocations, also known as assisted migrations, are highly controversial due to the danger of introducing invasive species.

The removal of trees without reforestation results in habitat and biodiversity loss. Also, forests are key locations for carbon storage so their loss means that more CO_2 remains in the atmosphere.

There is much that we do not understand about each functioning ecosystem. A lot of research is required before undertaking a relocation project—and still there are risks. Under some circumstances, a managed relocation can save a species from extinction, but in other cases, a relocated species can overpopulate its new habitat and cause the extinction of native species.

Such risks have traditionally compelled scientists to reject managed relocation as an option for conserving endangered species. However, many scientists are reconsidering this option as climate change impacts more and more habitats at an alarming rate, and endangered species do not have enough time to adapt.

Recycling glass, cans, plastic, and paper
products reduces greenhouse-gas
emissions. It also keep our beaches clean.

Chapter Six

What You Can Do

Climate change is already visibly impacting animal life in the United States and around the world. The choices we make now will determine the severity of its impacts in the future. Experts urge immediate action to address the causes of climate change, including a reduction in emissions from burning fossil fuels. This could slow down the rate at which habitats warm, protecting many animals from extinction.

There are many ways in which you can take action to slow climate change. Learn more about how climate change is affecting animals around the world, and then share your knowledge with friends, family members, and classmates. Encourage them to make simple changes in their lives that will help the environment.

▓ BE A SMART SHOPPER

Whether you're shopping for food, clothes, or other items, try to keep the environment in mind.

- Look for products made from recycled materials. These items reduce the need to harvest more natural resources, which means fewer greenhouse gases are emitted.

- Purchase sustainably farmed vegetables, fruits, fish, and meats. Sustainable agriculture improves the environment, uses resources efficiently, and works with natural biological cycles. Your local farmers' market is a good place to find sustainably farmed foods.

- Check out consignment shops for inexpensive and unique clothing. Most stores sell cool vintage pieces and unworn or lightly worn clothing and accessories.

- Buy wood products that have the FSC logo. This means they are accredited by the FSC, or Forest Stewardship Council, an organization that certifies only products whose manufacture does not endanger the world's forests.

▓ RECYCLE AND REUSE

Recycling reduces the need for landfills and incinerators, and it conserves natural resources. Many products we use today can be recycled, including aluminum cans, plastic containers, paper, and clear glass. Recycling items means fewer greenhouse-gas emissions are produced in the harvesting and manufacturing of natural resources. Check with your town or city to find out what the recycling procedures are for your area. Many retailers and organizations offer programs to recycle cell phones, computers, and other electronics so they don't end up in landfills.

Composting is a great way to put yard trimmings and food by-products that normally end up in the trash, such as banana peels, to good use. Compost naturally enriches soil, reducing the need for chemical fertilizers, which can pollute the ocean. Also, the manufacture of chemical fertilizers releases greenhouse gases that contribute to climate change.

You can also help the environment and slow climate change by finding new uses for old items, such as using an empty glass bottle as a flower vase. This keeps items out of landfills, thus reducing greenhouse-gas emissions.

USE LESS ENERGY

Little changes in your daily life, such as using energy-efficient lightbulbs, might not seem like much, but when lots of people make these changes, the effect is significant. Carpooling or taking public transportation reduces the amount of greenhouse gases being emitted into the air. Even air-drying your clothes instead of using a dryer saves energy, which means fewer greenhouse-gas emissions.

GET INVOLVED

If you'd like to do more to combat climate change, consider joining an environmental group. Check and see if there is an environmental club at your school and, if not, ask a teacher to help you start one. You will meet classmates who are also concerned about the environment and want to work together to make a difference.

You can also look at what programs in your school promote the reduction of fossil-fuel emissions. Most schools have a recycling program that includes paper, glass, aluminum, and plastic. Encourage your classmates to recycle, since all of these products can end up littering habitats. If your school has a cafeteria, look at how the food is packaged. Are the containers recyclable? If not, ask a teacher to help you find out if it's possible to use recyclable containers.

You can help prevent the extinction of species by working with other people who have a lot of experience in conservation. Join an environmental organization that helps protect animals and their habitats. These are four excellent organizations:

 350.org—www.350.org

 The World Wildlife Fund—www.worldwildlife.org

 The Nature Conservancy—www.nature.org

 Friends of the Earth—www.foei.org

Check out these websites to learn how you can join!

Glossary

Bergmann's Rule Rule stating that body size increases with latitude and tends to be smaller in the tropics; also known as the *temperature-size rule*.

biodiversity The variation of living organisms within an ecosystem or on the entire Earth.

biolink zones Areas that link one conservation area to another, allowing for the free passage of species.

biomes Major ecosystem types, such as forest, desert, grassland, and tundra.

biosphere The geographical region of Earth in which life is found.

biotope A small, well-defined area that is uniform in environmental conditions and its distribution of plant and animal life.

climatologist A scientist who studies climate.

desiccated Completely dried out.

ecological interaction The complex relationship between species in an ecosystem.

ecologist A scientist who studies the behavior of organisms—how they interact with the environment and with each other—including the distribution and size of populations.

ecosystem A group of living and nonliving things that interact with each other.

forage To search for food and provisions.

greenhouse gas A gas, such as carbon dioxide, that prevents heat from escaping Earth's atmosphere, contributing to global warming.

habitat The natural environment in which a species lives.

incubation period The time between exposure to a pathogen and the onset of symptoms.

invasive species Animals, plants, or insects that are not native to a given area and threaten the area's ecosystem and native species.

keystone species A species that plays a critical role in the structure and diversity of an ecosystem.

metabolic rate The rate at which an organism's metabolism functions, determining how quickly it burns calories and therefore how much food it requires to survive.

paleoecology The study of ancient ecosystems.

pathogen A disease-causing agent of some kind, especially a microorganism such as a bacterium, virus, or fungus.

phenology A branch of science dealing with the relationship between climate and key life events for species in ecosystems, such as bird migration and plant flowering.

physiology The study of the function of living things.

primary production Production of compounds through the photosynthetic process of absorbing carbon dioxide and producing oxygen, principally by organisms such as green plants.

range The geographic area in which a species or group lives.

terrestrial Living on land.

topography The surface shape and geological features of an area.

viral encephalitides Viruses that cause inflammation of the brain (encephalitis). Most viral encephalitides are transmitted by mosquitoes.

Notes

p. 5, Time to Act Fact, "The exhalations . . .": James Lovelock, *The Vanishing Face of Gaia* (New York: Basic Books, 2009).

p. 7, "Many animals . . . extinction.": Gary Braasch, *Earth Under Fire: How Global Warming Is Changing the World* (London, England: University of California Press Ltd., 2009).

p. 9, Time to Act Fact, "We depend . . .": James Leape, WWF Director General, Interview, *Planet Earth*, DVD (BBC Worldwide Ltd., 2006).

p. 9, Time to Act Fact, "The value . . .": Robert Costanza et al., "The Value of the World's Ecosystem Services and Natural Capital," *Nature* 387 (1997): 253-260.

p. 10, "Warmer temperatures are expected . . .": Jonathan A. Patz et al., "Global Climate Change and Emerging Infectious Diseases," *PubMed* 275, no. 3 (1996): 217-223.

p. 11, "The Sahara desert . . .": Erica Westly, "Warming May Radically Change Ecosystems," *Discover*, July 2007, http://discovermagazine.com/2007/jul/its-the-end-of-the-world-as-we-know-it-and-i-feel-warm#.UT8HUqWb2Ik.

p. 13, "Range shifts are being . . .": Camille Parmesan and Gary Yohe, "A Globally Coherent Fingerprint of Climate Change Impacts Across Natural Systems," *Nature* 421 (2003): 37-42.

p. 14, Time to Act Fact, "A recent study . . ."? Christopher Raxworthy et al., "Extinction Vulnerability of Tropical Montane Endemism from Warming and Upslope Displacement: A Preliminary Appraisal for the Highest Massif in Madagascar," *Global Change Biology* 14, no. 8 (2008): 1703-1720.

p. 14, "For species that live . . .": Scott Loarie et al., "The Velocity of Climate Change," *Nature* 462 (2009): 1052-1055.

p. 15, "Many North American birds . . .": A. Townsend Peterson and Enrique Martínez-Meyer, "Pervasive Poleward Shifts Among North American Bird Species," *Biodiversity* 9, no. 3 & 4 (2008): 114-116.

p. 15, "Many European bird . . .": Nathalie Doswald et al., "Potential Impacts of Climatic Change on the Breeding and Non-breeding Ranges and Migration Distance of European Sylvia Warblers," *Journal of Biogeography* 36 (2009): 1194-1208.

p. 17, Time to Act Fact, "Audubon's 2008 . . .": BirdLife International, "Birds' Movements Reveal Climate Change In Action," *ScienceDaily* 26 (February 2009), www.sciencedaily.com/releases/2009/02/090220191837.htm.

p. 17, "At least four hundred . . .": Walter Jetz, David S. Wilcove, and Andrew P. Dobson, "Projected Impacts of Climate and Land-Use Change on the Global Diversity of Birds," *PLoS Biology* 5, no. 6 (2007).

p. 17, "Observations made over . . .": Camille Parmesan, "Ecological and Evolutionary Responses to Recent Climate Change," *Annual Review of Ecology, Evolution, and Systematics* 37 (2006): 637-669.

p. 20, "Rising spring temperatures . . .": *IPCC Fourth Assessment Report: Climate Change 2007 (AR4)* (Geneva, Swizerland: United Nations Intergovernmental Panel on Climate Change, 2007).

p. 20, "Research shows that . . .": Parmesan, 2006.

p. 20, "According to studies . . .": Scott Norris, "Hibernating Animals Suffer Dangerous Wakeup Calls Due to Warming," *National Geographic*, February 2, 2007, http://news.nationalgeographic.com/news/2007/02/070202-groundhog_2.html.

p. 25, "Studies of aquatic . . .": Martin Daufresne et al., "Global Warming Benefits the Small in Aquatic Ecosystems," *Proceedings of the National Academy of Sciences* 106, no. 31 (2009): 12788-12793.

p. 26, Time to Act Fact, "Arctic foxes . . .": Pall Hersteinsson et al., "Effect of Sub-Polar Gyre, North Atlantic Oscillation and Ambient Temperature on Size and Abundance in the Icelandic Arctic Fox," *Global Change Biology* 15, no. 6 (2010): 1423-1433.

p. 27, "Milder winters . . .": Arpat Ozgul et al., "The Dynamics of Phenotypic Change and the Shrinking Sheep of St. Kilda," *Science* 325, no. 5939 (2009): 464-467.

p. 29, "Many are gradually . . .": Josh Van Buskirk et al., "Declining Body Sizes in North American Birds Associated with Climate Change," *Oikos* 119, no. 6 (2010): 1047-1055.

p. 29, "The changes in body size . . .": Janet Gardner et al., "Shifting Latitudinal Clines in Avian Body Size Correlate with Global Warming in Australian Passerines," Proceedings of the Royal Society B 276 (2009): 3845-3852.

p. 32, "It was 1987 . . .": Martha Crump, *In Search of the Golden Frog* (London: University of Chicago Press, 2000).

p. 32, "It wasn't long before . . .": J. Alan Pounds and Martha L. Crump, "Amphibian Declines and Climate Disturbance: The Case of the Golden Toad and the Harlequin Frog," *Conservation Biology* 8, no. 1 (1994): 72-85.

p. 32, Time to Act Fact, "There are only . . .": Mark Stanley Price, Chief Executive of Durell Wildlife Conservation Trust, Interview, *Planet Earth*, DVD (BBC Worldwide Ltd., 2006).

p. 35, "Scientists with . . . ecosystems": *IPCC Fourth Assessment Report: Climate Change 2007 (AR4)* (Geneva, Swizerland: United Nations Intergovernmental Panel on Climate Change, 2007).

p. 35, "Studies in Madagascar . . .": *IPCC Fourth Assessment Report: Climate Change 2007*.

p. 36, List, "Other animals threatened . . .": Wildlife Conservation Society, *Species Feeling the Heat: Connecting Deforestation & Climate Change* (Wildlife Conservation Society, 2009).

p. 40, "Studies have shown . . . of change": Jodi A. Hilty, William Z. Lidicker Jr., and Adina Merenlender, *Corridor Ecology: The Science and Practice of Linking Landscapes for Biodiversity Conservation* (Washington, DC: Island Press, 2006).

p. 41, "The loss of . . .": Edward O. Wilson, *The Diversity of Life* (New York: W. W. Norton and Co., 1999).

p. 42, "The mountain pygmy . . .": Dean Heinze, *25 Years in the Tunnel of Love: Habitat and Social Re-connectivity of the Endangered Mountain Pygmy-possum* (Melbourne, Australia: Department of Sustainability and Environment, 2009).

p. 43, Time to Act Fact, "As the world . . ."? *IPCC Fourth Assessment Report: Climate Change 2007.*

p. 44, "These urban networks . . .": Takuro Odawara et al., "Urban Ecological Network: Ecological Corridor Function of the Greenery in a City," *Technical Research Report of Shimizu Corporation* 83 (2006): 25–36.

p. 46, "Drought conditions . . .": *IPCC Fourth Assessment Report: Climate Change 2007.*

p. 47, "According to the U.S. Global . . .": U.S. Global Change Research Program, *Global Climate Change Impacts in the U.S.*, 2009, http://www.globalchange.gov/what-we-do/assessment/previous-assessments/global-climate-change-impacts-in-the-us-2009.

p. 47, "Water supply could . . .": Lovelock, 2009.

p. 47, "Climatologists fear . . .": U.S. Global Change Research Program, *Thresholds of Climate Change in Ecosystems*, 2009, www.globalchange.gov/whats-new/264-thresholds-change-ecosystems.

p. 48, "Forests (including . . .": D. A. C. Manning, "Biological Enhancement of Soil Carbonate Precipitation: Passive Removal of Atmospheric CO_2," *Mineralogical Magazine* 72 (2008): 639–649.

p. 48, Time to Act Fact, "The rise of sea . . .": Jim Robbins, "Between the Devil and the Deep Blue Sea," *Conservation*, April–June 2009, http://www.conservationmagazine.org/2009/04/between-the-devil-and-the-deep-blue-sea/.

p. 49, "However, many scientists . . .": David Richardson et al., "Multidimensional Evaluation of Managed Relocation," *Proceedings of the National Academy of Sciences* 106, no. 24 (2009): 9721–9724.

Find Out More

Books

Cherry, Lynne, and Gary Braasch. *How We Know What We Do About Our Changing Climate: Scientists and Kids Explore Global Warming.* Nevada City, CA: Dawn Publications, 2008.

Flannery, Tim, and Sally Walker (adaptation). *We Are the Weather Makers: The History of Climate Change.* Somerville, MA: Candlewick Press, 2010.

George, Charles and Linda. *Climate Change Research* (Inside Science). San Diego, CA: ReferencePoint Press, 2010.

Johnson, Rebecca L. *Investigating Climate Change* (Discovery!). Minneapolis, MN: Lerner, 2009.

Websites

Audubon Christmas Bird Count
Details are available on how to get involved in the Christmas Bird Count tradition and make an important contribution to bird conservation. Join other citizen scientists, experience the beauty of nature, and make a difference.
www.audubon.org/Bird/cbc/

Children and Nature Network
This site provides a lot of resources to make it easy to connect with nature programs near you. The mission of the Children and Nature Network is to build a movement to reconnect children and nature.
www.childrenandnature.org/movement/campaigns

National Geographic KIDS

Learn about some amazing animals, from giant pandas to great white sharks. Watch animal videos, play games and activities, and read animal stories. You can also pick up some green tips on how to protect the planet and share them with your family and friends.

http://kids.nationalgeographic.com/kids/animals/

National Wildlife Federation Wildlife Watch

This program is a great way to learn about the wildlife and plants in the area in which you live. Click on your state and find photos and information on animals, plants, and insects that you probably never knew were right in your backyard. Submit your observations, tell your story, and find out what other wildlife watchers have observed, too!

www.nwf.org/WildlifeWatch/

Will Steger Foundation Emerging Leaders Program

The main goal of this organization is to inspire a new generation of climate leaders around the world. Browse the climate-action partnerships, and see how you can raise your climate awareness.

www.willstegerfoundation.org/programs/emerging-leaders

World View of Global Warming

A picture is worth a thousand words. Put together by author-photographer Gary Braasch, this site is full of powerful photographs depicting the impacts of climate change all over the world. There is also plenty of information on current climate news and the impacts of climate change on specific regions of the world.

www.worldviewofglobalwarming.org

Index

Page numbers in **bold** are photographs, illustrations, and maps.

About the Author

Stephen Aitken is fascinated by the natural world and its remarkable diversity. He is the author of many books for young people from third grade to high school, written for publishers all over the world. Aitken is a biologist and senior editor of *Biodiversity*, a peer-reviewed science journal, and executive secretary of Biodiversity Conservancy International. He is a vegetarian, does not own a car, and tries to keep his carbon footprint as close to his shoe size as possible. Aitken's studio in the beautiful Himalayas of India provides shelter for ants and spiders, baby geckos, and an odd orange-eared mouse. For a complete list of books Aitken has written and illustrated, please visit www.stephenaitken.com.